For Lily — Stella Blackstone
To my three girls, Isabel, Sophie and Charlotte — S. B.

Barefoot Books
124 Walcot Street
Bath BA1 5BG

This book was typeset in Providence
The illustrations were prepared in fluid acrylics on 140lb hot press paper

Graphic design by Louise Millar, London
Colour separation by Bright Arts, Singapore
Printed and bound in Singapore by Tien Wah Press Pte Ltd

This book has been printed on 100% acid-free paper

Hardback ISBN 1-84148-493-8

British Cataloguing-in-Publication Data:
a catalogue record for this book
is available from the British Library

1 3 5 7 9 8 6 4 2

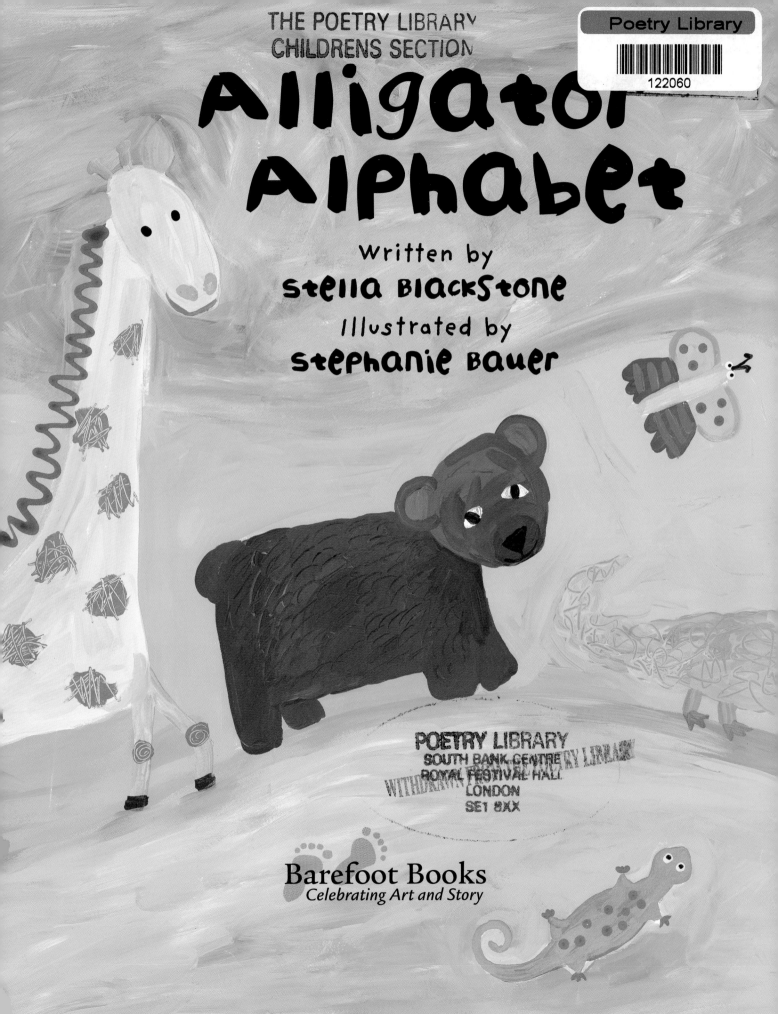

Alligator Alphabet

Written by
Stella Blackstone

Illustrated by
Stephanie Bauer

Barefoot Books
Celebrating Art and Story

Aa is for alligator.

Bb is for bear.

Cc is for camel.

Chase us if you dare!

Dd is for dolphin.

Ee is for emu.

F f is for fox and

for fish and ferret too.

Gg is for giraffe.

Hh is for horse.

I i is for iguana

and impala too of course!

Jj is for jaguar.

Kk is for kangaroo.

Ll is for llama

and for lion too.

M m is for monkey.

Nn is for newt.

Oo is for owl.

We hunt and we hoot.

P p is for panda.

Qq is for quail.

Rr is for rabbit.

We have tufty white tails!

Ss is for sloth.

T t is for trout.

Uu is for umbrella bird.

We like to fly about!

Vv is for vulture.

Ww is for wolf.

X x is for xoona moth.

We flutter as we move.

Yy is for yak.

We have long, shaggy hair.

Z z is for zebra.

We gallop here and there!

Now you know your alphabet
all the way through,
Can you name the letters
on the next pages too?

Barefoot Books
Celebrating Art and Story

At Barefoot Books, we celebrate art and story with books that open the hearts and minds of children from all walks of life, inspiring them to read deeper, search further, and explore their own creative gifts. Taking our inspiration from many different cultures, we focus on themes that encourage independence of spirit, enthusiasm for learning, and acceptance of other traditions. Thoughtfully prepared by writers, artists and storytellers from all over the world, our products combine the best of the present with the best of the past to educate our children as the caretakers of tomorrow.

www.barefootbooks.com